A QUESTION OF GEOGRAPHY

A QUESTION OF GEOGRAPHY

JOHN BERGER
AND
NELLA BIELSKI

faber and faber
LONDON · BOSTON

First published in 1987 by
Faber and Faber Limited
3 Queen Square London WC1N 3AU

Photoset and printed in Great Britain by
Redwood Burn Limited, Trowbridge, Wiltshire

British Library Cataloguing in Publication Data

Berger, John
A question of geography.
I. Title II. Bielski, Nella
822'.914 PR6052.E564

ISBN 0-571-14993-6

To the memory of
Yevgeniya Semyonouna Ginzburg

June–August, 1952
We chose this moment because it was one of relative quiet, of routine; ten months before Stalin's death. The last massive wave of arrests had been in 1949. Things were returning to 'normal'. The trauma of the war was a few years away. The economic situation was improving.

Kolyma
Region of the labour camps in the north-east of eastern Siberia, about 250 miles east of Oimiakon, where the coldest winters are regularly recorded. The river Kolyma crosses this mountainous landscape which is rich in seams of gold ore, and flows into the frozen Arctic ocean. The whole region is cut off from the rest of the country by mountains and the vast *taïga*. The only way in or out is by plane or boat. That is why the inhabitants call the rest of Russia 'the mainland' or 'the continent'. Kolyma is not, geographically speaking, an island; but to live there is to be exiled off-shore.

The one large town of the region is Magadan: the capital of the Gulag. (The word *Gulag* is an abbreviation in Russian for State Authority for Camps.) The area, with its capital city, was at that time a state within a state, with its own administration and population, the latter consisting mostly of Zeks, ex-Zeks and their guards, named collectively 'the Bruise'.

Thus Magadan and Kolyma exist in a very real physical sense; but their names also exist in the dreams and the unconscious of the Soviet people. For example, when Vissoski sings in one of his songs: 'I'm through – through with everything and I'm going to catch a plane to Magadan,' the words ignite memories and experiences which are beyond a given place and are larger than any individual. Such words are more than symbols: they form part of a history that has entered a people's soul.

Convit
(Combined vitamin.) A concoction made from pine needles, which contain vitamin C, thought to be an antidote against scurvy.

Sudar Lumbercamp
An area in Kolyma where prisoners were sent to fell trees. Given the cold, the lack of food and warm clothing, a stint of work there often proved fatal. Being sent to Sudar was a disciplinary measure, a punishment, meted out particularly to '58s'.

'A 58'
A term used to describe any prisoner, man or woman, condemned under Article 58 of the penal code. This article was interpreted so loosely that it finally covered all prisoners who were not criminals by common law.

Article 58
The 14th paragraph of this article enumerated all activities subject to being considered prejudicial to the interests and security of the state. They ranged from 'spying' to 'terrorism', from 'sabotage' at work to a refusal to denounce other 'traitors'. Under this article anybody could be condemned if picked upon. A '58' was spoken of as 'an enemy of the people'. In the camps they were treated worse than ordinary criminals.

Zek
A popular abbreviation of *zaklioutchonny*, meaning prisoner.

The Bruise
A name invented for the military personnel in charge of the camps. In fact they were known as 'Vokhra' which is an abbreviation from *Voorujonnaïa Okhrana*, meaning armed guards. For us *the Bruise* also includes those who worked for the KGB (Committee of State Security). The latter wore blue insignia on their uniforms. From this blue came the colour of the bruise.

A Decembrist
After the mutiny of officers against the Czar on 25 December

1825, in St Petersburg, the term *Decembrist* came to mean a revolutionary or idealist. Pushkin celebrated them in his poetry.

The Taïga
This is very different from the steppe. It refers to the enormous Siberian forest area which supplied wood for the whole of the Soviet Union. In Stalin's time nearly all this wood was felled by prisoners. Nothing romantic resided in the word *taïga*.

NELLA BIELSKI

CHARACTERS

ERNST MOISSEEVITCH OIZERMANN

Nicknamed 'Eric' by Daria. Forty-six years old, thin, with curly white hair. Limps slightly. He wears a worn, shiny suit. Metal spectacles. He carries everywhere a battered, leather medical bag. His situation in Magadan is unlike that of any of the other characters. He is still a prisoner in the Zone, but, because he is a doctor who treats the guard officers, he has a right to come into the town during the afternoons.

DARIA PETROVNA PETROVA

Abbreviation: 'Dacha'. Thirty-eight years old. She is not particularly beautiful, but she has a strong, reassuring presence. The reassurance she gives has a lot to do with her gestures. She was arrested in 1937 and served ten years in the Zone. Now she is in permanent forced residence in the town of Magadan. She works in one of the town's infant schools. Dacha and Ernst met in the Zone. They live, as best they can, as a couple.

SACHA

Sixteen years old. The son of Dacha. He was one and a half when his mother was arrested. He has been brought up in Leningrad by Dacha's sister, Katya. Like all boys of his age – and despite his size and adult appearance – he reveals a mixture of maturity and childishness.

GRICHA

Sixty years old, bald, agile – with something of the conjurer about him, something of the fox. He has seen more of the Zone than anyone else. Now in Forced Residence. He works as a porter in the special stores for the Bruise. (The Bruise is the term used to designate guards, officers and all Zone administrators.)

IGOR ISSAIEVITCH GERTZMANN

Fifty-five years old. Once a violinist of great talent. His body, although aged and worn, still suggests this. He wears a quilted coat and canvas trousers – almost the same as he wore as a Zek in the Zone. In Forced Residence.

LYDIA IVANOVNA
Forty-three years old. Slightly over-dressed – in hand-me-down clothes. An economist by training. Worked, before being arrested, in the planning section of a textile factory. An amateur 'expert' of literature and poetry.

MICHA
Thirty years old. He was in the Zone as a criminal, not as a political prisoner. Now works as a lorry driver. Is free to leave and return to the Continent.

UNKNOWN YOUNG WOMAN
Between twenty-two and twenty-five years old.

BRUISE 1
Forty years old. A little tired and slack in his duties.

BRUISE 2
Younger than Bruise 1. Handsome, tall, zealous.

A Question of Geography is set in Dacha's room, in Magadan, the principal town of Kolyma. It covers the period June–August 1952.

A Question of Geography was first performed in French by The National Theatre of Marseille in 1985 at the Theatre of the Criée, and, later, at the Odéon in Paris. It was first performed in English by the Royal Shakespeare Company at The Other Place, Stratford-upon-Avon, in 1987. The cast included:

ERNST MOISSEEVITCH OIZERMANN	Clive Russell
DARIA PETROVNA PETROVA (DACHA)	Harriet Walter
SACHA	Linus Roache
GRICHA	Jimmy Gardner
IGOR ISSAIEVITCH GERTZMANN	John Carlisle
LYDIA IVANOVNA	Susan Colverd
MICHA	Peter Polycarpou
UNKNOWN YOUNG WOMAN	Sonia Ritter
Director	John Caird
Designer	Sue Blane

ACT ONE

SCENE ONE

June 1952. Evening. It is still light. (Outside, the white night of the Arctic.) A room in an apartment house in the port of Magadan, principal town of Kolyma. The room, on the ground floor, is large and very simply furnished, but one senses in it the presence of a woman. On the left a window, on the right the door on to the street, two beds, a table, a sink. DACHA – *apron, chignon, wearing glasses – is reading a book at the table. There is food ready on the table: potatoes, herring, black bread. A lamp, shaded with an orange scarf.* DACHA *is waiting. On a massive primus stove a 50-litre saucepan of water is simmering. On the floor is a zinc bath.* DACHA *looks up towards the door, then at a large alarm clock. We hear the tick-tick loudly.* ERNST *opens the door with his own key and enters.* DACHA *takes off her glasses and watches him come towards her. He limps slightly. He places on the table a string bag with two newspaper packages inside it. Then he opens his case and takes out a stethoscope, and an old instrument for taking blood pressure.* DACHA *rolls up her sleeve. No word has yet been spoken. He takes her blood pressure. Meticulously.*

ERNST: Sixteen. It was seventeen yesterday, no?
DACHA: On Monday I had nineteen.
ERNST: I want to keep it at sixteen. For a 58/11, aged 38, that's not bad. (*Puts away his instruments, goes to wash his hands.*) Six terminal cases today. Three scurvys, sent to the hospital, and two TBs. It's a good omen. The Bruise may be getting more human.
DACHA: Perhaps good omens are still possible. Who knows?
ERNST: A 58/10 will probably die during the night. If I can manage some sleep . . .
DACHA: You have to sleep. Who is he?
ERNST: A poet.
DACHA: You saw his file?
ERNST: Yes, I remember his name – Serebriakov.
DACHA: (*Nodding*) Pavel Serebriakov.

ERNST: (*Unwrapping the newspaper packages in the string bag*) Look, some greengroceries.

DACHA: Not a present from the poet!

ERNST: (*A little grimace*) They're straight from the Agrobase. The Colonel called me out again this afternoon. His daughter has measles. Mother and Father were beside themselves; they thought their little daughter had scarlet fever. I reassured them. So they gave me a lettuce.

(ERNST *eats the bread for a moment without speaking.* DACHA *watches him, as she does every evening, listening to the recital of his day.*)

As for the Colonel, since his arrival, there are two conflicting points of view about him. Some say he is scrupulous but sadistic; others say he is sadistic but scrupulous! I don't take sides. By his little daughter's bedside he fusses like a hen. My diagnosis of measles earned me the lettuce and radishes.

DACHA: The Colonel is generous!

(ERNST *finishes eating and is more relaxed. He comes behind* DACHA *and puts his hands on her shoulders. She leans her head back against his chest.*)

ERNST: Twelve visits in the town this evening. Eleven of them for nothing. The twelfth had cirrhosis of the liver. A sergeant of twenty-five, drinking himself to death. I warned the Colonel that in the Zone Operating Theatre we have no gauze left. We have to sterilize rags. I told him even twenty kilograms of gauze would be something to go on with. It'll make no difference.

DACHA: (*Smiling*) And do you know what I want to go on with?

ERNST: What?

DACHA: Twelve square metres of hardboard.

ERNST: What?

DACHA: And if that's not possible, twelve square metres of thick cardboard.

ERNST: Nobody could say you lack imagination, my love.

(ERNST *starts to undress. His white body is badly scarred.* DACHA *pours water into the bath.*)

DACHA: You have teeth like Gary Cooper.

ERNST: Thanks to the pine needles! By the way, *convit* is no longer obligatory, a new order from Moscow.

DACHA: You'll always be the most beautiful man in my life, and the pines have nothing to do with it.

(ERNST, *naked, walks over towards the window.*)

ERNST: What's the hardboard for?

DACHA: Patience, doctor, patience. Everything in good time. Come.

(ERNST *sits in the bath.* DACHA *soaps and washes him.*)

The last time I saw Sacha I was bathing him. There was a knock at the door. I wiped my hands on the apron. (*Imitates the gestures.*) There were four of them. What's it for, I asked. I knew what it was for. My own worry was who was going to finish giving Sacha his bath. They're thoughtful, the Bruise; they had already warned the neighbour's wife.

ERNST: And now your Sacha knows *how* to bath himself and doesn't need you for that.

(*She is soaping his hair.*) But me (*laughs*) I do!

(DACHA *pours water over his head. Both are laughing. There is a knock on the door.* DACHA *makes the same gesture with her soapy hands on her apron and goes to half-open the door. A* BRUISE *pushes it wide open.*)

BRUISE I: Citizen Oizermann.

ERNST: (*Sitting in bath, still naked, calm*) Citizen Oizermann present! (*To* DACHA) Give me my glasses. (*Puts them on. To* BRUISE I) What can I do for you?

BRUISE I: You are required to report immediately to the Commandant.

(*He approaches the bath, stiffly.* DACHA *seizes a towel and holds it up like a curtain, so as to hide* ERNST. *The* BRUISE *– ill at ease – ignores the towel.*)

ERNST: You want me to come like this?

(*He stands up, dripping naked.* DACHA *tries to raise the towel higher.*)

BRUISE I: You have five minutes. (*Turns abruptly and strides back to the door.*) The Colonel's daughter has vomited up her supper.

(*The* BRUISE *leaves.* ERNST *steps out of the bath and starts dressing.*)

DACHA: Too much to eat!

ERNST: (*Dressing quickly*) Calm, Dachenka. Don't fret. Why do you want the hardboard?

DACHA: A telegram came today.

ERNST: From whom?

DACHA: Leningrad.

ERNST: Bad news?

DACHA: From Sacha.

ERNST: Sacha!

DACHA: That's why I want the hardboard.

ERNST: Dacha, I have to go, don't talk in riddles.

DACHA: Sacha has taken the decision to come to Magadan.

ERNST: Taken the decision!

DACHA: When the school year is over.

ERNST: This year?

DACHA: In about a week.

ERNST: What time?

DACHA: Eric, he's coming, he's coming here!

ERNST: And the hardboard?

DACHA: To make a room for him in the corner there.

ERNST: It won't happen.

DACHA: (*Still holding the towel in her hands*) I believe he will come.

ERNST: May God protect him and may he never come here!

(ERNST *goes towards the door. Pauses. Takes a wrapped sweet out of his pocket.*)

The Colonel's other child gave me a sweet. (*Pause.*) Keep it for Sacha.

DACHA: It'll be a good summer, Eric, you'll see.

(*Exit* ERNST. DACHA *starts to empty the bath. Stops in mid-action and takes the telegram out of her pocket. Reads it out loud.*)

'Decision taken by Sacha to spend vacation in Magadan. Stop. Letter follows. Stop. Katya.' You were bigger than me, Katya, and more serious and more beautiful, yet you were jealous. You couldn't be jealous of me now, Katinka, could you? It wouldn't be reasonable.

(*She picks up the zinc bath to hang it on the wall. The light from the window is fading.*)

Every time Maman said it was bath time you howled so loud,

Katinka. Papa would come out of his study and say: Be quiet, Miss. The Great Blanqui, Miss, is just about to make his speech to the massed crowd at Bourges on the 15th May 1848, how can I follow such an historical moment with you making this din? How could we know then, Katya, that following historical moments would earn him a bullet in the neck?

(*Through the window a patriotic song sung by passers-by who are drunk. And the voices of a man and woman quarrelling.* DACHA *shuts the window angrily. She picks up the sweet from the table and turns it in her fingers.*)

'Decision taken by Sacha.' So you take decisions, you are almost a man.

(*She sits down on the bed by the door. The light from the window continues to grow fainter. Pause. Ticking of clock.*)

Your father used to come, Sacha, and fetch me after my lectures. He would wait by the bridge and we'd cross it together. He always carried my books. He had very blue eyes, like yours, full of light. He had tiny feet and wore pointed shoes – as if he wanted to have the least contact possible with the ground.

(*Pause. Ticking.*)

He somehow saw us all and the whole history of our planet from way, way above, from where everything fitted together perfectly into circles and the circles into spirals going higher and higher. The great hymn of history!

(*Clock.*)

When I told Papa I was going to marry Serioja, Papa made a joke: So your children will be young Hegelians! How could we know that studying Hegel with passion would lead to six millimetres of pointed steel in the back of the neck.

(*Pause. Ticking.*)

Before we knew that, before they arrested your father, he never liked it when I wore black. When you're very young, wearing black gives you the idea of being a *femme fatale*.

(*Knock on the door. Enter* GRICHA. *He enters the room like a conjuror beginning his act.* DACHA *switches on the lights. He holds a herring wrapped up in paper, as if it were a bouquet of flowers. He embraces* DACHA.)

GRICHA: Hedgehogs are the only animals who make love looking at each other face to face. Don't argue. I've just seen them doing it. My compliments! The only woman of Magadan who stays the same. (*Unwraps the paper to display the herring.*) Fished off Vladivostock! It's not Swedish, it's not Norwegian, it's not Icelandic – this fish was caught in the waters of Holy Russia! Fat, juicy, and the spices, oh, the spices that go with it – cinnamon, bay leaves, cloves, nutmeg, peppercorns – all, like perfumes on the breath of our motherland! Ten barrels full. Do you have a cigarette? I unloaded a ton of tomatoes today. Don't look surprised. If the cases drip, we say they're loaded with tomatoes. (*Still holding the herring*) Take it, sweetheart, it's not a stinging nettle. Grasp it firmly from underneath, move the hand up – never down – and it won't sting.

DACHA: Gricha, haven't you been drinking?

GRICHA: We'll never know when the ball is over.

(*He begins to dance with the herring clutched to his chest.* DACHA *intervenes, takes it from him and puts it on the table.*)

DACHA: Better dance with me!

(*They waltz a few steps. Abruptly* GRICHA *steps back.*)

GRICHA: Fuck it! I've never seen you dance before, not even when you got your White Pass.

DACHA: My son's coming.

GRICHA: Children are the flowers of life! And who is the Best Friend of All Children, everywhere?

DACHA: Be quiet!

GRICHA: There! You've given yourself away. No wonder they picked you up and did you with Article 58. You are incorrigible, you refuse his edification – he who is the Best Friend of All Children, the Best Trainer of All Athletes, the Great Linguist.

DACHA: Anyway he's coming.

(GRICHA *takes out of his pocket a small bunch of daisies and places them beside the fish on the table.* DACHA *watches, a little indulgent.* GRICHA *sits on the bed by the door. Suddenly he looks tired. Silence. We hear the clock.*)

GRICHA: You haven't got a cigarette to give me?

(DACHA *finds him one on the shelf with the books.*)

DACHA: Gricha, dear, can you lay your hands on some hardboard and a little door?

GRICHA: You should catch the rabbit before you build the hutch!

DACHA: This rabbit is now sixteen.

GRICHA: And what the fuck is he coming to do here?

DACHA: Everyone tells me the same thing. What's the matter with you all? Even Ernst.

GRICHA: I'm sorry. It was a hard day.

(DACHA *clears the table. A calm.*)

DACHA: How's the pain in your chest, Gricha?

GRICHA: (*Ignoring the question*) You must be wondering how your son will feel about Ernst.

DACHA: I suppose so.

GRICHA: Forget it. More to the point to ask how he will feel about all of us here in the white frozen fog. One should never underestimate the importance of geography.

DACHA: (*Quietly and almost to herself*) If he took the decision – that's what it said – read it!

(*She takes the telegram from her apron pocket and hands it to him. He holds it far away for he is far-sighted.*)

GRICHA: 'Imprudent decision taken by Citizen Dacha, to ignore geography. Stop.'

DACHA: He never knew his father.

GRICHA: Let us consider Ernst as Father Elect. Ernst was born to be a father.

DACHA: Perhaps yes . . .

GRICHA: If you want to have a large family you must know how to count. Counting comes naturally to our Ernst Moisseevitch.

DACHA: (*Very quietly*) I saw him, one spring morning in the Zone, counting the number of leaves on the one and only tree.

GRICHA: It must have been a snowball tree.

DACHA: Why?

GRICHA: 'Where there's a snowball tree, there's always an uncle' as the proverb says. A variety of viburnum . . . And your Sacha, he lives with his uncle?

DACHA: Yes, the husband of my sister, Katya. He's an architect who has built two universities.

(*Silence. Clock.* DACHA *goes to the bed behind the curtain and sits down on it to sew. We can see both* DACHA *and* GRICHA *but to each other they are invisible. They speak across the curtain. For a little while they let the silence continue:* DACHA *sewing,* GRICHA *sinking into fatigue.*)

Gricha, why did the Bruise let me go that night at Agrobase number 5?

GRICHA: I told him you had syphillis. And I ought to know! I told him. I made out I was one of your victims.

DACHA: (*Murmuring*) You were my guardian angel.

GRICHA: He didn't want to believe me. He said that on the list of Zeks there was nothing about the clap against your name. It's just happened I told him, since the last examination. And cunt that he was, he believed me.

DACHA: You should have been a diplomat, Gricha, not a porter at the Special Provisions Depot.

GRICHA: You're right and what's more I speak French like a Frenchman. 'Dans l'orient désert quel devint mon ennui!' Racine!

DACHA: They suffered in Racine too . . . At Agrobase 5 I never thought I'd live to see Sacha.

GRICHA: Miracles only happen in this world, Dachinka, not in the next . . . (*Slumps into fatigue and then comes to life again.*) Take the miracle of the Holy Trinity. For two millennia it had them worried, and it is only now at the beginning of the fifties of this century, so full of promise, that your Gricha has discovered the secret. I am my own Father, my own Son and my own Holy Ghost.

DACHA: (*Leaving the bed and approaching him*) I think the Holy Ghost has had enough. Supposing he sleeps here tonight?

GRICHA: Do you know I saw – with my own eyes – two cases of oranges today.

DACHA: Can you get some for Sacha?

GRICHA: There's always a grass about.

DACHA: Don't run the risk, then.

GRICHA: I never run risks. I'm untouchable.

(DACHA *leaves* GRICHA *sitting on the bed. She goes to the mirror and undoes her hair, which falls over her shoulders. She goes to the bed behind the curtain.*)

DACHA: Goodnight, Gricha. Sleep well.

GRICHA: (*Sitting on the bed, his head between his hands*) Goodnight . . . Goodnight . . . those must be the words they still repeat on the Continent before they are arrested. Goodnight, sweet dreams, the shits of this motherfucking motherland . . . sssshhh, Gricha, ssshhh, my little boy, sshh, papa, goodnight, my boy, goodnight, papa, goodnight motherfuckers. (*Takes off his socks and shoes and brings one of his maimed feet to his mouth, kisses it.*) There's the cleverest . . . ah! . . . the brains of the foot. (*Strokes and cradles one of his feet. Then lies down, murmuring*) Shh! Sshh! Goodnight . . . sshh.

(*The lights go down. We hear breathing in the dark.*)

SCENE TWO

A week later. Evening. The scene unchanged except that in the far left corner a partition with a door has been put up to make a room for Sacha.

MICHA: (*In the doorway, reluctant to enter*) I'll be leaving you here. This is where she lives.

SACHA: (*Entering*) Come in, there's no one here, come in. (*He looks round the room, surprised and curious.*)

MICHA: You feeling a bit lost, little brother?

SACHA: A bit.

MICHA: Take it easy, they've seen everything here. You'll find a place for yourself.

SACHA: I was meant to arrive tomorrow, you see, that's why there's no one. I came today because tomorrow's flight was cancelled. (*Pause.*) So she lives here. I've seen a photo of her, a marriage photo, but nothing since.

MICHA: In the Zone, kid, there aren't any picture-framers.

SACHA: She has dark eyes and she's not very tall. She'd come up to my chest, I'd say.

MICHA: I've never seen your mother. I've just heard about her. She works at the Infant School.

SACHA: What have you heard? (*He walks round the room examining the few objects.*)

MICHA: You'll have so much to tell each other, the summer won't be long enough. (SACHA *opens a small wooden-framed triptych leaning against the wall and reads the title of one of the pictures, invisible to the audience.*)

SACHA: *Flight into Egypt* by Nicolas Poussin. (*Pause. Looks up at* MICHA.) What brought you here?

MICHA: The legal system.

SACHA: And now?

MICHA: I could leave for the Continent tomorrow, if I wanted.

SACHA: (*Holding up Dacha's apron*) Why don't you?

MICHA: Sometimes I ask myself that question when I'm in bed. The pay's good here.

SACHA: It isn't the same for my mother. She can't leave.

MICHA: Don't forget, little brother, your mother is listed as an Enemy of the People.

(ERNST *appears in the doorway*.)

ERNST: You've come! Dacha was expecting you tomorrow. Was the door open?

MICHA: Yes, doctor, the door was open.

(*He holds his cap in his hands*.)

ERNST: Wait! She'll be here.

(ERNST *disappears hurriedly*.)

SACHA: Who's he?

MICHA: He's your stepfather.

SACHA: How?

MICHA: Your mother's been with him for about seven years, I think.

SACHA: They aren't married?

MICHA: I wouldn't know, but they met in the Zone, and there aren't any wedding dresses in the Zone.

SACHA: You called him 'doctor'?

MICHA: One of the rare good ones, Uncle Ernst Moisseevitch. Uncle Permanganate we used to call him. Poor sod, he's still got five years to do.

SACHA: How's that? You say he lives here, with my mother.

MICHA: In the afternoons, Ernst Moisseevitch treats the Bruise . . .

SACHA: The Bruise?

MICHA: The Bruise are the law here. He treats some of them and their families. That way he often gets a free pass out of the Zone into the town until eleven o'clock at night. (*Pause*.) He's gone to fetch your mother now, so I'll be off.

SACHA: How did they meet there – inside?

MICHA: Don't ask me. It's rare you can get away with it. For 58s love is listed as a crime.

(*A knock at the door*. LYDIA *enters carrying a saucepan. Having put down the saucepan, she pointedly ignores* MICHA *and goes straight to* SACHA.)

LYDIA: One didn't hope to see you here so soon.

SACHA: Nor did I.

LYDIA: Your mother's great day! For years she never dared to hope to see you again! All she could take with her, when she was transferred under escort, was your name . . . Sacha. Nobody could steal that from her.

(LYDIA *glances reproachfully at* MICHA. ERNST *enters, smiling. He strides across to* SACHA *still carrying his medical bag. He taps* SACHA *on the chest, a caricature of a chest examination.*)

ERNST: Fit. Congratulations. How on earth did you get here?

MICHA: I picked him up at the airport.

ERNST: You have a vehicle? (*Examines* MICHA *more closely.*) Haven't I seen you before?

MICHA: From time to time I deliver medical supplies.

ERNST: Yes, yes, a free worker. What article were you convicted under?

MICHA: Nothing special. Pickpocketing.

ERNST: Ah! An artist!

(LYDIA *starts to prepare food in the kitchen corner.* SACHA *looks a little confused.* GRICHA, *a Lenin cap on his head, an orange in his hand, enters like a whirlwind.*)

GRICHA: Our Prodigal Son has returned! Get out those trumpets, you stomping archangels! The horses are coming, the angels are marching in! Everybody outside! Line up! The Prodigal Son has returned. (*Pauses and politely shakes* MICHA*'s hand. Then, to* SACHA) Down on your knees. (SACHA *remains bewildered but self-possessed and standing.*)

Everybody down on your knees. The sweetness of the mother's breast, the authority of the father's hand on the son's head! The family home with all modern conveniences, gas, electricity, running water. Oh, the miracle of running water, hot and cold!

(DACHA *enters, taking off her scarf.* GRICHA *does not see her; his back is to the door. Nor do* LYDIA *or* ERNST. *But* SACHA, *looking over* GRICHA*'s shoulder, sees her immediately and cannot take his eyes off her.* DACHA, *as if mesmerized in her* *turn, leans against the doorpost staring back at her son.* GRICHA'*s speech of welcome does not stop. The light outside is fading.*)

Long live all miracles! Never again to limp out of bed into the skimmed frozen milk of the fog. Never to be knocked over and held down by the dogs! It's finished now. Well and truly over. Long live all fairy tales! Warm yourself, little one, by the radiator. May milk and honey melt in your mouth.

(*As if he has sensed the presence of* DACHA, GRICHA *turns towards the door.*)

May honey melt in your mouths. Madonna and Child!

DACHA: (*Still leaning motionless against the doorpost*) Dear Gricha, let us be.

(*The others busy themselves with laying the table and arranging the chairs. Mother and son, still divided by almost the entire width of the stage, watch each other, smiling. The lamp on the table is switched on. There is another knock on the door. Enter* IGOR. *He bows formally to* DACHA, *as if to an audience.*)

IGOR: I was passing and I saw a light through the window . . . what a public occasion it is. Daria Petrovna! Your home is so full of people.

DACHA: (*With a gesture of her hand*) Igor Issaievitch, my son has come home.

(IGOR *crosses the stage like an ambassador from* DACHA *to* SACHA *and embraces him.*)

IGOR: May you always return like this, this the first time! By aeroplane or by dream, no matter the means of transport, may you always return like this.

(*Everyone is moving and talking at once. We can barely distinguish their words.* LYDIA *brings on a saucepan of soup.* DACHA *puts bottles on the table.* GRICHA *makes a few dance steps by himself.* MICHA *protests that he must go, and* GRICHA *insists that he stay.* ERNST *leads* SACHA *to a place at the table and everyone sits down. The chair next to* SACHA *is left vacant for* DACHA. *She is the last to sit down. She touches* SACHA'*s cheek, her hand slowly descending to his chin.*)

DACHA: You've shaved.

SACHA: Yes, I shave now.

GRICHA: And supposing we drink? Red for the ladies, white for the gentlemen.

(*He pours the bottles. Hesitates before* SACHA*'s glass.*)

And what will the Continent drink?

SACHA: The Continent likes vodka.

(DACHA *puts her hand over the glass to prevent* GRICHA *serving* SACHA *vodka.*)

ERNST: Let us drink to Daria Petrovna's and Sacha's happiness!

DACHA: And yours, Eric.

SACHA: And my father's!

GRICHA: To be alive at all is a sin.

(*They drink.*)

IGOR: How fine the soup is.

LYDIA: There's wild sorrel in it.

ERNST: An official order came this morning. *Convit* is no longer compulsory.

GRICHA: Everyone struggles for himself. It's obligatory.

SACHA: What is *convit*?

ERNST: A concoction made from pine needles, that everyone in the Zone is obliged to eat before the evening meal.

LYDIA: It makes you want to vomit and it takes away even the appetite of the famished. They invented it to punish us.

IGOR: Sorrel, I believe, was almost a sacred plant for the Greeks. It cured so much.

ERNST: The Academy of Medicine in Moscow has decided that whatever little good *convit* does to compensate for a lack of vitamins, it has disastrous effects on the liver. It killed thousands.

DACHA: Eat, Sachinka.

ERNST: And now we are going to be spared *convit*.

GRICHA: Ah! The perspicacity of the Academy of Medicine!

ERNST: Serebriakov, the poet, died this morning. He was reciting a verse, it was addressed to a woman called Maria. I asked him if it was an old poem. A new one, he replied.

SACHA: What did he die of?

ERNST: Alimentary dystrophy on his papers. In reality internal bleeding from the beating-up during interrogation.

LYDIA: 'They taught me the science of goodbyes in the wild sobs of the night.'

SACHA: Who?

ERNST: (*To* SACHA) Lydia Ivanovna is a specialist of our poetry in the so-called Silver Century.

(GRICHA *starts to touch* SACHA*'s shirt and jacket as if he were a buyer in a shop. He takes his own cap from the back of his chair and puts it on* SACHA*'s head.*)

GRICHA: The Silver Century! And our Kolyma so rich in uranium!

ERNST: (*Again to* SACHA) And Igor – Igor Issaievitch Gertzman – is a violinist. He won the First Prize in the International Concours of Vienna in 1932.

IGOR: What Ernst says, young man, is not quite true. I am no longer a violinist.

LYDIA: You will play again.

(GRICHA *imitates a violinist.*)

IGOR: Never!

SACHA: You could play if you wanted to, or don't I understand?

IGOR: How can you understand? Unless I tell you more . . . When I was first transferred to the Zone, I had a stroke of luck. I caught typhus. Hospitalized, in quarantine, sheets, food, nurses. After the going over I'd had in Lubyanka, it was like a paradise. I could almost imagine a Stradivarius in my hands. And it was there, there in hospital, that I learned the habit of playing concerts to myself. You decide on the programme – Bach Prelude in F minor, 'Death and the Maiden', a Mozart concerto – and then you start. And with all those bars in your head, you forget the barbed wire, you forget everything else.

LYDIA: 'Of Russia's monstrous years we are the offspring . . .'

DACHA: Eat, Sacha.

ERNST: Lydia Ivanovna . . .

LYDIA: (*To* SACHA) Chief of the Planning Section for the Red October Textile Factory in Kharkov. Arrested for sabotage of the national economy.

SACHA: (*To* IGOR) So why don't you play?

IGOR: In 1939 I was transferred to a logging camp at Arkagala. There is such a silence in the *taïga*. I caught an ear infection which lead to a tympanosclerosis. But what is partial deafness for a musician? Nothing. It was the music itself which was slowly leaving my soul. It was too cold, the silence was too heavy, there was nothing inside me.

ERNST: At minus 40 Centigrade and with 400 grams of bread a day . . .

IGOR: I had a friend. He slept for a while on the bunk above mine. In his other life he had been a professor of comparative religion, Professor Vassiliev. He talked to me about how he envisaged the sacred. I listened to him and I watched the fog. And then one day I suddenly heard the sense of his words and to hear this sense was like listening to another kind of music. A music that nobody can play. (*Pause.*) He had a book in English – Vassiliev – God knows how he got it. It wasn't a whole book, just part of a book, without a cover. Written by an Englishman called Fraser. I inherited this book from him along with a scarf, knitted by a woman whom Professor Vassiliev greatly loved. For the Professor died. He had great endurance and it was he who taught me my endurance. Yet he died. He died from the same disease as Serebriakov.

GRICHA: (*To* SACHA) No music there and no sense. It's pure geography.

MICHA: You're right. In the *taïga* not much sense. There's this mate of mine, he's a lorry driver too. Picked up in 'forty-seven for slaughtering his uncle's pigs. He meets a girl here in Magadan, she's a 58 in Forced Residence, like Daria Petrovna here. Liola, that's her name, and she lives in Pioneer Street. Slim, dark, with eyes like almonds, that's Liola. When he meets her, this mate of mine, she's pregnant, with no father around. So he does everything for her. Buys her a bed, buys a bath tub, buys clothes for the baby-to-be. He'd drive anywhere in the *taïga* so long as it earned him a bonus he could spend on Liola.

(SACHA *leans forward to hear this story.* LYDIA *is obviously disapproving.*)

What happens? He comes to the depot one morning and he's told to load six fucking drums of barbed wire. Where for? he asks. They tell him it's for Arkagala, where they're building a new Zone. It's a long way and there's a bloody great bonus. Transport that shit! he shouts. Never will I take that shit! We all try to reason with him. Useless. There, on the spot, the Bruise pick him up. He's back in the Zone now, this time as a 58. And where's the sense in what he did? Shouting off his big mouth?

ERNST: Perfectly correct. There's always somebody ready to unroll the barbed wire.

MICHA: I delivered it myself. Why not? And the bonus I earned, I gave it to this Liola. She was weeping her heart out for her hero. Kept on calling him her 'Decembrist'. What's that? I asked. She explained to me that it meant a Villain who changes into a hero! I look at her and think: my poor girl, where's the sense?

ERNST: Has she had her baby?

MICHA: Last month, a girl. We decided to call her Alice.

LYDIA: The water's boiling.

ERNST: Your Vassiliev, Igor, was his first name Kostia? He must be the same one. I was once in the same hut with him. He used to tell stories at night to the Villains, and they paid him with bread and protection.

IGOR: Yes, he was one of the most sought-after novelists . . . Scott, Victor Hugo, Gogol . . . He could keep twenty men quiet. Once, I remember, he refused to go on with *The Count of Monte Cristo* and, instead, he told a story which haunted me for a long time.

SACHA: Why?

IGOR: A strange story.

LYDIA: I'll serve the tea.

IGOR: When he'd finished, the Villains swore at him, and ordered him to go on with *The Count of Monte Cristo* the next night.

ERNST: Tell us the story, Igor Issaievitch.

IGOR: I've never told it before?

LYDIA: No.

IGOR: Once there were a people who were forgotten by the rest of the world. Perhaps they were not entirely forgotten, but they believed they were. The world fell silent, they themselves – this people – fell silent. And then one of them, a puny man who had lost most of his teeth, said: Let's go and look for the Beginning; like that, at least we'll be moving, instead of squatting here like fools. And so they set out. Quite soon they saw the walls of a city where there were great houses, palaces, temples. They said to themselves: Perhaps this city is the Beginning. As soon as they entered it, they were overcome by the stench and everywhere they stumbled over carcasses, all black and swollen. They left the city and continued on their way. Nothing got better. They crossed rivers red with blood, they crossed battlefields. They saw burned villages smoking. On and on they went, discouraged, more discouraged than when they started. Suddenly the puny man, who had lost most of his teeth, stopped and announced: We have arrived! Behind this hill is the Beginning! Behind the hill they found a small tower, broken down and useless, and a field of earth, freshly ploughed. Nothing else at all. Only one thing was strange: the sky, above the earth, didn't join the rest of the sky, it was like a separate miniature sky, set apart and on its own. So that's all there is to the Beginning! the people muttered, an acre of earth and its sky like an old hat! People need many miracles before they believe in one.

DACHA: (*Quietly*) And one miracle can make many seem possible.

IGOR: They'd had enough of travelling and forced marches and they said: We'll start again from here as if it was the Beginning. Only the puny man kept wondering about who had ploughed the earth before they came. The others set to work. They cut down the forest, they quarried, they made roads, they built towers which were useful. And as time went on, the miniature sky, above where the field had once been, grew and grew, until it was completely absorbed into the large sky. Everybody forgot about the Beginning, a regular routine set in, and nobody wondered any more about how anything began . . .

(*Silence. Nobody reacts visibly to the story. We hear the clock.* DACHA *gets up, takes the clock from the shelf and holds it up for* ERNST *to see.*)

ERNST: I must be going. My nightly routine . . .

(ERNST *picks up his bag, strokes* SACHA*'s head.* DACHA *accompanies him to the door.*)

IGOR: I talk too much. It is so rare that we have a visitor from the Continent. Forgive me, my friends. Goodnight, Sacha. Shall I walk back home with you, Lydia Ivanovna?

(IGOR *leaves the table, accompanied by* LYDIA.)

ERNST: (*Standing by the door, addressing* IGOR *and* LYDIA) So the two of you are leaving together for a little duet!

LYDIA: Me?

ERNST: It's never too late to begin!

MICHA: (*Getting to his feet, to* SACHA) Beyond me his story – but Liola will understand it. I'll tell her. You know where I hang out, if you need me.

GRICHA: (*Taking his cap*) Welcome to Magadan, Sacha. The feet are the most intelligent part of the human body.

(*Everyone goes out of the door, saying goodbye.* SACHA *is alone. He sits at the table, head in hands. He visibly makes an effort, raises his head, searches in his jacket pocket, and produces an envelope which he places on the table.* DACHA *returns and sits beside him.*)

DACHA: Look at your plate, you've hardly eaten anything. (*Notices the envelope.*) Where did this letter come from?

SACHA: It's for you.

DACHA: From Katya?

SACHA: (*Slowly*) No. It's from my father – or, if you like, it's from your husband.

DACHA: (*Overwhelmed*) From Serioja!

(DACHA *takes the letter, unopened, and goes over to the window, standing with her back to* SACHA.)

It must be an old letter.

SACHA: No. It's dated the 8th May 1952.

(DACHA *speaks to* SACHA *but with her back turned to him, in order to hide her face. Her voice is low as if addressed to herself. Nevertheless she is speaking to* SACHA.)

DACHA: The last news I ever had of him was at the public desk of the Cross prison on the 15th November '37. 'Transferred with no right of mail.' Those were the words. And they meant: Serioja had been executed. I'd heard the same words applied to Father in October . . . (*Turns to face* SACHA.) You must be exhausted after such a full day. *Full day!* (*Catches her breath. Walks towards him.*) You see the little room? When we knew you were coming, we built it for you.

SACHA: (*His mind elsewhere*) It wasn't necessary.

DACHA: There's a basin and a jug of water to wash your hands and face.

(*They are standing close, face to face.*)

SACHA: And my feet?

DACHA: (*With infinite tenderness*) And your feet!

(*They embrace. For an instant* SACHA*'s shoulders collapse, and his head falls on to her breast. Almost immediately he straightens up and holds her at arm's length.*)

SACHA: I've come, Mama.

(SACHA *goes into his room.* DACHA *returns to the window, pensive. Lights fade.*)

Come here for a little while, Mama.

DACHA: Yes, my son, I'm coming.

(*Darkness.*)

ACT TWO

SCENE I

A fortnight later. Early evening. SACHA *is alone. On the table a bunch of wild flowers and a bottle of milk.* SACHA *is wearing different clothes, more in keeping with life in Magadan. He opens the window, fetches a vase of water, arranges the flowers in it, glances at himself in the mirror, combs his hair. Enter* DACHA.

DACHA: So the nightbird is at home for once!
(*She takes off her shoes by the door and puts on slippers.*)
A surprise today! The local radio station is going to broadcast something from our play at the infant school.

SACHA: What's it about?

DACHA: (*Laughing*) In our version the Wolf doesn't really eat the Grandmother! The Wolf meets Little Red Riding Hood and goes with her, like an escort, to Grandma's Convalescent Home.

SACHA: Does the Wolf look like the Bruise?

DACHA: Of course not.

SACHA: You surprise me! (*Holds out the vase of flowers towards her.*) Not for the Wolf and not for the Grandmother, but for you!

DACHA: (*Smiling*) Is the nightbird staying in tonight? It's days since we've seen you, Ernst and I.

SACHA: I'm nearly seventeen now! And think of the years I've lived through, not just any seventeen years – 1936 to 1952. Just think what he has seen, your son!

DACHA: We have to wait nine months, my little one, before you are seventeen.

SACHA: The Great Patriotic War, the Great Victory, the Transition from Socialism to Communism . . . I've seen more than you have.

DACHA: And you are still sixteen!

SACHA: That's a detail. When I didn't come home, you knew very well I was at Gricha's. Last night I was back by quarter to one. I walked with Ernst Moisseevitch as far as the Zone. Eight kilometres, there and back.

DACHA: How was it you met Ernst? He didn't come last night, yet I wasn't worried, as I would have been once.

SACHA: The worst is over, Mother.

DACHA: How much you remind me of Serioja.

SACHA: Do I?

DACHA: You look up in the air when you're telling a story, just like Serioja.

SACHA: Like this?

DACHA: Tell me, Sachinka, how did you meet Ernst last night?

SACHA: That's a story in itself, a Magadan story. What I like about being here is that I meet so many people . . . and one of the places where I meet people is the Continental.

DACHA: It's a kind of hotel.

SACHA: Hotel! You see how you need a sixteen-year-old to tell you about Magadan!

DACHA: That I need you, yes, Sacha.

SACHA: It's a hotel for Zeks who've just got their release and who are waiting to go to the Continent. An extraordinary place, a real club for gentlemen, nothing like your crummy Cultural Centre.

DACHA: There's a library at the Centre with books that are unfindable anywhere else.

SACHA: I met a number at the Continental who speaks six languages, and has been all round the world.

DACHA: So far?

SACHA: It's not far, it's in a little street that leads down to the Nagaiev Bay, close to the sea, it's a basement, well-heated – well, it's even suffocating this weather, very large. Where else can they go, your Zeks? They can't all have super love affairs with great doctors. So they hang out there. Greenhorns who have just been released, others who can't make up their minds whether to go or stay, all of them waiting for their boat to come in – mostly they aren't in Forced Residence, like you. It's a real museum, the Continental. Kids, babies, women doing their washing, cooking, singing. Little groups of men talking – talking about really serious things. Girls too, plenty of girls with nail varnish and even permanent waves! All this just a stone's throw from the sea. It must be strange in the winter when the waves on the bay are frozen.

DACHA: Winter is what's normal here, it's these two months now, the months you are here, which are abnormal.

SACHA: There's a girl called Helena who has a super voice. Gypsy love songs she sings, you can't believe it. And do you know, she offered, just like that, she offered to teach me to play the guitar.

DACHA: (*Putting her hand to her forehead*) Really?

SACHA: (*Oblivious of the effect his words are having on his mother*) I've chatted with some hard cases. Tough guys. Men who really committed crimes against the State, not a question of words like most of you. Hard cases if you like, but they're not bone-headed. They think things out, they plan carefully. To hijack a cargo ship for instance. The guards are always pissed, so it would be child's play to disarm them . . .

DACHA: (*Her hand to her heart*) Stop, Sacha!

SACHA: (*Suddenly aware of his mother*) I never drink anything there, Mother, except tea, and I never go there alone. I never go there without Micha.

DACHA: And what sort of record does Micha have? There are drug-pushers, there is venereal disease, and worst of all, worse than you can ever imagine, there is the Bruise.

SACHA: I never go without Micha.

DACHA: That doesn't reassure me.

(*The light begins to dim, slowly, as the evening draws in.*)

SACHA: What have all you 58s got against Villains? They're victims like you.

DACHA: The Villains and the Bruise speak the same language.

SACHA: And that, Maman, is what I'm trying to learn something about. Yesterday I talked to a 58 – a Party Secretary of the district of Saratov. Ten years inside and they've changed absolutely nothing for him. He sits in the Continental with a red pencil, correcting the articles he reads in the *Kolyma Red Star*. And he's convinced that, since he had served his sentence for the 'regrettable error' he made in 'thirty-seven, he will now be able to continue his career in the Party and make up for lost time.

DACHA: (*Almost to herself*) So many lost times . . .

SACHA: If only you could meet Ignatiev! There's a hero – a man tempered like steel, as they say in school. Ignatiev was a ship's captain of a large ocean-going freighter. At the beginning of the war he was transferred to a cruiser of the Baltic Fleet. He fought the Germans off Leningrad, fought like a tiger. Only when it was hopeless did he break the German blockade and get his ship and crew safely to Sweden, where they were interned until 'forty-five. After the victory he requested to be sent home. Request accorded. The rest you can imagine. Now that he is out, he won't be had a second time! He'll get away, he has the sea in his blood, Ignatiev.

DACHA: 'Fathers can be found anywhere', that's what your father wrote to me in his letter, remember? 'My one wish,' he said, 'is that Sacha may one day rejoin you.' Be careful, Sacha!

SACHA: Don't think he's a dreamer, Ignatiev, he has it all worked out. Alaska is no distance from here. You'll see, they'll make it to America!

DACHA: When you walked with Ernst back to the Zone last night, what did you talk about?

SACHA: About God. Why do you ask? (*Looks at the clock.*) Isn't he late?

DACHA: What?

SACHA: Ernst, Maman! Look at the time.

DACHA: Don't worry. Half an hour, an hour late, is nothing. He's not always his own master. I'll put on the supper. (*She switches on the table lamp.*)

SACHA: Can you imagine Ernst Moisseevitch as he was when he was young? When he was my age?

DACHA: Yes, easily, just as I can imagine you in twenty-five years' time . . .

(*Enter* ERNST *with his newspaper packets. He switches on the ceiling light. He looks and acts tired. He salutes* SACHA, *and then, straightaway and without a word, as in the first scene, he takes* DACHA*'s blood pressure.*)

ERNST: Twenty.

(*He goes to wash his hands and takes too long about it.*)

DACHA: Don't worry, Eric.

(*They sit down.* DACHA *serves the soup.*)

SACHA: When you were my age, Ernst Moisseevitch, did you know you wanted to be a doctor?

ERNST: Yes, I did. When I was younger still, I dreamt of being a sailor.

(ERNST *sees* DACHA *taking some salt to put into her soup.*)

More salt! No, Dashinka, not in your condition.

DACHA: I've been learning things about the sea of Okhotsk this evening, Eric.

ERNST: Icebound for seven months of the year.

DACHA: It's child's play, it seems, to cross it and go to America.

ERNST: How's that?

DACHA: By boat, of course!

SACHA: Via Alaska . . .

ERNST: (*Drily*) Ah yes! I see. I never thought of that.

(*He stops eating.*)

DACHA: How was your day?

ERNST: Eventful. (*Takes off his glasses and puts them on again.*) Last night I was called to the Continental – a heart case. I gave the man an injection and who should I see but our poet here (*nods towards* SACHA) drinking tea in company. We left together and he accompanied me back to the Zone. (*Again takes off his glasses.*) When we came out of the hotel, I noticed one of the Bruises' lorries and I said to myself; a routine check up. Better, I thought, for Sacha not to be there when the Bruise arrive, you never know, but in general they turn a blind eye to most of what goes on at the Continental. I was mistaken. Do you know what happened after we left? They pulled in your entire tea party – they're inside now – Ignatiev and all his pals.

SACHA: I don't believe it! Ignatiev is too smart to get arrested for nothing!

ERNST: I suppose the ideas about the Sea of Okhotsk came from your tea party?

DACHA: (*Putting her head between her hands*) Eric, how to tell him, how to explain to him?

(SACHA *gets up and goes to stand by the window.*)

For a whole hour he's been telling me stories about hijackings, heroes, Alaska, escapes. Everything is like an adventure film to him. What can we do? What can we say so that they understand?

ERNST: (*Very calm*) Our lives here, Sacha, can never be a film, never. We have lost many things, things that people take for granted elsewhere. And one of the most important things we've lost is the right to be seen. Everything we live has become invisible. (*Switches on the lamp on the table.*) Even if, by some miracle, somebody made a film of our lives here in Kolyma, all that would be seen on the screen would be a blizzard, with visibility reduced to a few metres. The blizzard of our losses. Nobody would be able to see the little we've managed to protect from the blizzard. The grains on which we live are invisible. You come here. I'm not sure what a boy of your age thinks. It's a very long time ago since I was sixteen. Probably you find us colourless, a peculiar mixture of passivity and nervousness.

SACHA: That's not true!

ERNST: I'm sure you believe that somehow we can choose. Choose like Ignatiev to put to sea and cross the Bering Straits! You are wrong. Ignatiev has been arrested. Here there are no choices – or no choices like you imagine.

SACHA: You're saying none of you have any choices!

ERNST: Everything outside forbids a choice. The choices we make are inside.

(*He indicates his chest. There is a pause.* SACHA *still beside the window.* DACHA *is sewing.* ERNST *is eating his soup, spoon in one hand.*)

When you drag yourself back after a day's work in the *taïga*, when you are marched back, half dead with fatigue and hunger, you are given your ration of soup and bread. About the soup you have no choice – it has to be eaten whilst it's hot, or whilst it's at least warm. About the 400 grams of bread you have a choice. For instance, you can cut it into three little bits: one to eat now with the soup, one to suck in the mouth before going to sleep on your bunk, and the third to keep until next morning at ten, when you're working in the

taïga and the emptiness in your stomach feels like a stone.
(SACHA *moves from his place by the window and goes towards the cooking stove.* ERNST *slowly gets to his feet.* DACHA *stops sewing and watches both the men.*)
You empty a wheelbarrow full of rock. About pushing the barrow to the dump you had no choice. Now it's empty you have a choice. You can walk your barrow back just like you came, or – if you're clever, and survival makes you clever – you push it back like this, almost upright. If you choose the second way you give your shoulders a rest.
(SACHA *moves again towards the bed.* ERNST *takes the chair on which he was sitting and places it close beside* DACHA, *before sitting down on it.*)
If you are a Zek and you become a team leader, you have the choice of playing at being a screw, or of never forgetting that you are a Zek.
(*Pause.* DACHA *puts a hand on his shoulder.*)
When I receive a new contingent of the dying I have a duty to look after them all as best I can. In addition, I have the *choice* of trying to do even more, of trying to do the impossible, for one of them whom I feel must be saved at all costs.

SACHA: (*Getting up and moving towards his room*) Why not all of them?

ERNST: Because I do not have the means to choose that. (*Pause.*) Here's us, your mother and I. Since 'forty-seven when Dacha got her White Pass, she couldn't choose to leave Magadan. But she could have chosen, she can still choose, to leave me. Me, a Zek with another five years to do.

DACHA: About love there is no choice . . . and I have only one son. Tell him, Eric.

ERNST: (*Going up to* SACHA) The Continental and its gang – you understand, Sacha, all that must stop. Once and for all, you understand? You can see how your mother is. Do you want to kill her?

SACHA: (*Angry*) What do you want me to do with my time? Who do you want me to see? The kids of your Bruise officers? You want me to arse-crawl with the Bruise? Or do you want me to kick my heels here all day whilst both of you are out working? Forced Residence for everyone!

(*He opens the door to his room, enters and slams it behind him.* ERNST, *equally angry, seizes the doorhandle and pulls it violently towards him to open it. The makeshift door comes off its hinges. He tries to put it back. Fails.* SACHA *remains invisible.* DACHA *comes to* ERNST*'s help. Together, solemnly, they carry the door across the stage and lean it against the wall, near the front door. When they turn they see* SACHA, *framed in his doorway, wearing a sailor's cap.*)

(*Smiling*) Never mind, I don't need the door. Without a door, we can communicate better, no?

DACHA: Your cap?

SACHA: A present from Captain Ignatiev.

DACHA: It quite suits you.

ERNST: You can't go out in a cap like that.

DACHA: (*Going up to* SACHA *and adjusting the cap on his head*) Like this.

SACHA: (*Indicating the alarm clock*) Look at the time, Ernst Moisseevitch. (*To* DACHA) Let's both go with him tonight.

ERNST: Not in that outfit.

SACHA: No, chief, without it.

(*He takes off the cap. All three exit. They leave the lights on. For a moment nothing changes on the empty stage. Then the lights begin to go down. A glass jug of water falls off the table. A mixture of distant sounds: wind, the shouts of guards, dogs barking. None of it is dramatic. What we hear are like the sounds of a distant play in another theatre. A beam of light falls on the middle of the stage. The rest in darkness. From the back of the auditorium a man's voice mixes with the other sounds and quickly dominates them. It is* SERIOJA*'s voice reading his letter.*)

SERIOJA: Dacha, my little darling, how to find the words now? Can you imagine, out of the darkness, out of the darkness of so many years, I received a letter from Katya. Like one of those flashes of light in Plato's cave. I learned that you are alive, that Sacha is almost grown up. How can such miracles happen? I have to pinch myself to make sure I'm awake. Yes, I am. Fifteen years! For fifteen years, too, I haven't

held a pen, so don't be hard on my handwriting. A guard fetched me this morning, brought me here to the office, gave me this pen and paper and said: You have the right of addressing one letter to your wife. And me, idiot that I am, I started to cry. Where are you, my little one? I go back and back to the bridge in front of the Hermitage. Each paving stone, each arch of the bridge which we used to cross together, you in your black dress with a satchel – all, all is engraved. We were always in a hurry – for we had to go and fetch Sacha. I have lost my teeth and I have lost the toes of both feet. Since three years I have been on the stoves in the bath house, a merciful job for I'm no longer cold. I don't have much appetite, which is just as well. I suck with my gums and eating takes a long time. I'm not like an old man, I'm more like an old child who has forgotten his age. Hegel used to say that the difference between a dead person and a child is that the child doesn't have a memory. There our philosopher made a mistake because he couldn't foresee an intermediate category: one who is neither newborn, nor old, nor dead, nor living, yet who has a memory. I always believed that the magic of your hands wasn't in your hands but was in the way your hands obeyed your eyes. You must have said I was dead and now I come back, alive! If I'm not transferred to the mines, I'll hold out, and you must go on thinking of me as dead, you will be closer, my heart, to the reality. My soul, my spirit, my memory have long since joined those of the dead who are, after all, the majority; and, in comparison with whom, the living are rare. Try not to think of me as being here, think of me rather as one who has already joined the Spirit of History which is watching over you from the furthest stars. I know every square millimetre of your body, astonishingly and eternally. My one wish is that Sacha may one day rejoin you. Fathers can be found anywhere. Know all this, my darling. As for me, I know it, and this knowledge is like a guiding star which will show me, until my last breath, where to place my frozen feet. We are already saved!
(*Everything on the stage resumes its normal appearance. Silence.*

Enter DACHA *and* SACHA. DACHA *takes off her scarf by the door.* SACHA *notices the broken glass jug and picks up the pieces.* DACHA *looks round the room, troubled, suddenly anxious.*)

SACHA: It must have been a draught. (*Shuts the window.*) The wind is getting up over the bay.

(DACHA *wanders vaguely round the room, touching things, a plate, a chair, the glasses. Rubs a finger round the rim of a glass, holds it up to the light. Suddenly decisive, she goes to the bookshelf, chooses a book and from between its pages takes out Serioja's letter. Sits down on a chair holding the letter to her breast.* SACHA *fetches a rag to wipe up the water under the table. After using it, he rolls up the rag, and starts to kick it around like a football.*)

DACHA: Go and see Gricha tomorrow, will you? He's picked up a tin of corned beef. Lydia is knitting a scarf and mittens for him. The winter will soon be here. (*Notices that she has crumpled the letter and now smooths it out on her knees.*) The first parcel must get to Serioja before November. By a miracle I got a whole salted cod today. He'll soak it in water to get rid of the salt and he'll eat it raw . . . it's very very good . . .

(DACHA *looks up at her son. He has stopped playing football with the cloth and, as if all his energy had gone, has fallen on to his knees. He sobs.* DACHA *stands behind him, her hands on his shoulders and neck and we see her, wordlessly, calming him.*)

SCENE 2

A few days later. Evening. SACHA *and* GRICHA *are sitting on two chairs, facing each other, in the middle of the room. Between them is a small table covered with a red rag. The evening lighting is not quite as usual. The small table is extra-lit, as if by a spotlight. The effect of a theatre within a theatre.* GRICHA *is wearing an artificial moustache, somewhat reminiscent of Stalin's. It is obviously attached by elastic.*

GRICHA: Are you going to confess?
SACHA: I've already said Yes.
GRICHA: In what town?
SACHA: Babylon.
GRICHA: With who?
SACHA: We were two.
GRICHA: Fucking lie. You were three.
SACHA: Not on that spree.
GRICHA: The third came from Prague.
SACHA: I'm just a bit vague.
GRICHA: Pure chicanery.
SACHA: A counter-revolution.
GRICHA: His name please!
SACHA: Diogenes.
GRICHA: Where did you meet?
SACHA: In Gorky Street.
GRICHA: This confirms what has been said.
SACHA: With how many blows to the head?
GRICHA: You scab, you sore, you blight on the people's body, listen to me. (*Approaches* SACHA.) When I pull on this chain, you stand up. When I pull a second time, you sit down. (*Pulls an imaginary chain, in the air by his right-hand shoulder.*) On to your feet!
(SACHA *gets up.* GRICHA *pulls on the chain again.*)
Down !
(SACHA *sits.*)
Stand! Sit! Stand!

(*Whilst* SACHA *is standing,* GRICHA *discreetly takes away the chair, resumes his place, pulls the chain.* SACHA *sits and falls to the floor.*)

You scabby shit – nothing, nothing will teach you! If there's no chair there, my sweet little one, you stay like this – just as if there was a chair! If I order you to sit, it means there's something to sit on! Let me see you sit.

(SACHA *sits on air, as if there was a chair there.* GRICHA *slightly corrects his posture with his hand.*)

All right, my monkey, you stay like that. Twenty-four hours on that chair and ideas will come to you by the hundred.

(GRICHA *sits down at his place behind the table.* SACHA *is sitting on air.*)

Now – I want the names of your accomplices.

SACHA: Come plis this way, come plis!

GRICHA: (*Furious, pulling the chain continuously*) Up! Down! Up! Down! Why did Diogenes offer you gum to chew?

SACHA: That's not true.

GRICHA: Shit! Do you think you can reply like that, you! The only negative reply we permit is: 'Not in my presence.'

SACHA: Not in my presence!

GRICHA: (*Standing up in his fury*) Do you want the ice bin?

SACHA: Frédéric Chopin.

GRICHA: At last a name!

SACHA: Do you prefer Schumann?

GRICHA: Schumann, Haussemann, Huissman! So you were seven.

SACHA: Yes, seven with Sunday.

GRICHA: That's better, you're learning how to play.

SACHA: We met on Fridays.

GRICHA: Traitors – (*Pretends to think.*) – Babylon – Prague – Diogenes – chewing gum – America – Chopin, Frédéric – the Bering Sea – Alaska – a conspiracy against the Cheka!

(*From under the table he picks up a raw herring and begins to slap* SACHA*'s face with it.* SACHA, *sitting on air, remains immobile.*)

Fascist! Organist! Archivist! Nationalist! Continental Tourist!

(*A knock at the door.* SACHA *stands up.* GRICHA *rips off his moustache, and stuffs it into his pocket. His haste indicates nervousness. He grabs the red cloth off the table and throws it under the bed.*)

Come in.

(*Enter* MICHA. *Not as we have seen him before. Pale, slovenly. He sits down on the chair where* SACHA *sat.*)

(*To* MICHA) You look as though you've had a real going over, my boy. Sacha, do we have anything in the First Aid Kit?

(*Silence.* SACHA *brings over two glasses and a bottle of unlabelled alcohol.*)

Neat or with water?

MICHA: Neat.

(GRICHA *pours out.* SACHA *fetches a plate of gherkins.* MICHA *takes a gherkin and knocks back his glass.*)

Where's your mum and dad?

SACHA: They've gone to the film of the week. Vivien Leigh and Robert Taylor, what is it called?

MICHA: You should have heard the dressing down your old man gave me the other day. About taking you to the Continental. It was like the wrath of God.

SACHA: I saw you yesterday on Stalin Avenue. You looked like somebody in a trance.

MICHA: They've picked up Liola.

SACHA: Arrested?

MICHA: Nicked.

GRICHA: Which Liola? Who is she?

SACHA: Liola – you don't remember? The girl of his mate, the lorry-driver, the girl who was pregnant. A 58 with almond-shaped eyes. The lorry-driver got arrested for talking out loud, and Liola was very proud of him. He was her Decembrist, she said.

GRICHA: (*Very precise*) When was she arrested, this Liola?

MICHA: They picked her up last night, at her place. She was feeding the infant. Alice. She called her baby Alice.

GRICHA: Yes. Yes. I see. So Liola has gone to join her Decembrist – as the poets used to say. How out of date these poets are today! Nobody joins anybody in the Zone.

MICHA: (*Quietly*) I'm going to wait for her.
GRICHA: Her? Who?
MICHA: Liola.
(GRICHA *fills up the two glasses. Hands one to* MICHA *and one to* SACHA.)
No, no, not for Sacha. Ernst Moisseevitch would kill me.
SACHA: (*Winking at* GRICHA *who drinks the glass in question*) Never in my presence! I don't understand, Micha. I just don't understand. Is it your mate or is it you who loves this Liola with almond eyes?
MICHA: Ten years, twenty years – I'm going to stay here in Kolyma and wait for her.
GRICHA: (*Sarcastically*) And you'll send her little parcels!
SACHA: Why not? We sent a parcel to Father today.
GRICHA: When your Liola comes out, she'll be a toothless old lady – supposing all goes well, and she behaves herself! And her Decembrist? What are we going to do about him?
MICHA: That's her business.
GRICHA: Who on earth is this Liola? A simple Villain becomes a knight in shining armour, under her spell.
SACHA: Who do you mean?
GRICHA: I'm talking about her Decembrist. And as for our poor Micha here – he was an honest thief and he's being transformed into a Don Quixote! All this for a pair of almond eyes. Ah Kolyma, Kolyma, land of paradise! If I was in your shoes, Micha, I'd have got the hell out of here long ago. I'd be in the south sun-bathing. You're not condemned like us to stay here for life, and you're young.
MICHA: Liola isn't the only one. They are picking up others too. There's a rumour they're going to arrest all the 58s for the second time.
GRICHA: (*Softly*) The third time for me. (*Pause.*) Your victim with the almond eyes – tell me – what's her name?
MICHA: Liola.
GRICHA: Liola *what*, for heaven's sake? Tell me her surname!
MICHA: Annissimov.
GRICHA: And the others they've arrested, do you know their names?

MICHA: No, I don't think so, let me think. In any case, what does it matter, if you don't know them? Hang on, yes, there's this bloke – he's lost an arm – lives just down the street from us, they arrested him this morning, and his name is Avevtchenko.

SACHA: What's happened to Liola's baby daughter? Alice, you said.

MICHA: She's been bundled off into an orphanage – the special one for the kids of the Enemies of the People.

GRICHA: Annissimov . . . Avevtchenko . . . Alice.

(*A knock on the door. Enter* LYDIA *and* IGOR. LYDIA *wears a smartish dress with a fox fur round her shoulders.* IGOR *has a white scarf over his usual jacket. As they enter* MICHA *gets up to leave.*)

IGOR: We were passing and we saw a light in the window . . .

SACHA: Come and sit down, make yourselves at home.

MICHA: I'm off . . . I have some mates waiting. (*To* SACHA) I really came to ask you something. Next week I'm doing a trip into the *taïga*. Supplies for a group of geologists working in the north, I've been there once, and they're mostly from Moscow. Come with me if you can, it'll be company.

SACHA: Is it far?

MICHA: About two hundred by road, and then a hundred cross-country.

SACHA: I'd like to come but you know how it is. I must ask Ernst Moisseevitch first. If he says yes, I'll come. Something else I thought of. Mother has a friend who works in the orphanage. Perhaps she could arrange for you to go and see Alice if you wanted to . . .

(MICHA *nods and exits without a word.*)

LYDIA: He looked as if he was in trouble, your criminal friend there, what is it?

GRICHA: Nothing, nothing at all.

IGOR: And you two, you look like conspirators of some sort. What's been going on here?

SACHA: Just an evening's theatre.

LYDIA: And do you know what we did tonight? We went to see a film. A real English melodrama, set in London of all places!

SACHA: Yes, with Vivien Leigh and Robert Taylor. My parents are there now.

LYDIA: We went to the earlier programme.

IGOR: Daria Petrovna and Ernst Moisseevitch will enjoy themselves. It's about a man who comes back from the war, wounded. His hair has gone white. The woman who was the great love of his life believes that he is dead. And in her grief and desperation, she has become – a fallen woman.

SACHA: Do you know, Igor Issaievitch, nowadays, such a woman is called a tart!

IGOR: One day they meet again and that's where the story begins. She is very beautiful, and he is an aristocrat. If I understood correctly. The strangest thing of all was that everybody at the Cultural Centre, sitting there in the dark, everybody was wiping their eyes and snivelling. The Bruise with their wives and children, and we who were once Zeks – and will probably be Zeks again – masters and slaves, we all reacted in the same way to this love story . . . there's a waltz in the film which is like a refrain. (*Hums it.*) My mother used to play the very same waltz at home when she gave dancing lessons. I can still see her fingers, very long and white, flying over the yellow keys of our piano, which was far from new, and her head bent forward and her fair hair rather untidy . . . The timbre of that piano was wonderful, a little dry, cold, metallic, just what I liked from a piano.

(*He hums the waltz again, louder than before.*)

GRICHA: Keep it up, Igor Issaievitch, keep it up! The moment has come for you to learn to dance a waltz, Sacha!

(*He pulls* SACHA *to the middle of the room and demonstrates the steps.*)

One . . . two . . . three – don't walk on my feet – one . . . two . . . three . . . you see . . . it's simple, simpler than an interrogation . . . one . . . two . . . three.

(*He makes* SACHA *turn faster.*)

You are gifted, my prince, that has to be said. One . . . two . . . three . . . you are gifted.

(LYDIA *takes* IGOR *by the hand and leads him to dance. All four dance and hum the tune.*)

LYDIA: (*To* IGOR) You haven't forgotten . . . you haven't forgotten anything.

(*She closes her eyes. A recording of their humming, with a piano added, now takes over as music.*)

IGOR: The waltz, with its unique rhythm, was, you know, an invention of the nineteenth century. According to Spengler, the tempo of the waltz corresponds exactly to the spirit of modern man . . . the same steps repeated but always at a new level . . . a kind of diagram in dance of the Hegelian dialectic.

(*He shuts his eyes and the two of them dance intensely.*)

GRICHA: Your son-of-a-bitch Hegelian dialectic has cost us something, and it's not over yet. To hell with your dialectic! And to hell with its mother and father!

(*The four dance with more and more verve, then slow down.*)

IGOR: No need to have it in for Hegel. If Marx hadn't taken his dialectic and turned it on its head . . .

GRICHA: We wouldn't all be here and Magadan wouldn't . . .

(SACHA *accelerates their movement so that* GRICHA *is forced to stop talking.*)

IGOR: (*Softly*) Surely we wouldn't be here.

(*The four are still dancing.*)

SACHA: You say Marx stood it on its head, but didn't he stand it on its feet? And that's how the dialectic became materialist . . . one . . . two . . . dialectical materialism.

LYDIA: (*Clinging very close to* IGOR) Sacha is right, what he says rings a bell. But before we were dancing so well . . . with or without a dialectic!

(*Out of breath,* LYDIA *stops and leads* IGOR *to the table. The music continues.*)

(*To the others*) We are going to give violin lessons.

IGOR: (*Drily and a little breathlessly*) Don't start again, I beg you, Lydia Ivanovna. It's out of the question. Music in all its forms is over for me, do you understand? Over, once and for all. And where I am now, in my little caretaker's room, with my notebooks and my little library, I am happy there. I earn a living and I have no boots to lick. I sweep the cinema, I pile up chairs, I regulate the radiators . . .

LYDIA: The lessons would only be for children.

IGOR: *Their* children.

(GRICHA *and* SACHA *are still dancing but* GRICHA *is out of breath.*)

GRICHA: Don't be so pig-headed, Igor, each of us has to live.

IGOR: I do live, thank you.

LYDIA: You live, you think you live! Your room is damp. You have how many broken ribs? You have rheumatism, Igorik! My room is sunny and twice as big. In your basement there's not even room for a double bed.

IGOR: My bed is still a bed, incomparably preferable to a bunk in the Zone.

(GRICHA *and* SACHA *have stopped dancing and the music dies away.* GRICHA *sits down.*)

GRICHA: It sounds like a family quarrel! Ah! How beautiful they were, those family quarrels!

SACHA: (*Sitting on one of the chairs of the 'Interrogation' scene in the middle of the room*) It's true, Igor Issaievitch, her room, the room of Lydia Ivanovna is better.

GRICHA: And what a good cook she is! What a housekeeper!

LYDIA: Will you all shut up please? We can settle this ourselves.

IGOR: (*Very gently and softly*) My bed is not a bunk.

GRICHA: Perhaps you ought to settle your affairs quickly.

LYDIA: Rumours, rumours, they're all we have to go by here. Yes, yes. There have been a few isolated arrests, I'm fully aware of that. But I have heard, and I have it from the highest authority, that a new wave of arrests is out of the question, there are going to be no mass arrests.

SACHA: Mass arrests. What does that mean? How many make a mass? How many Zeks are there on the planet of Kolyma?

LYDIA: Many thousands.

IGOR: A mathematician I knew in the Zone – who was an expert in statistics in his first life – made his own calculations about the population of our planet. For a while he worked as a clerk in the administration. According to him it was between 3 and 4 million.

LYDIA: (*Lowering her voice*) Igor, please, it's better not to be heard quoting numbers.

IGOR: No statistics and no music lessons!

(*A long silence. Sound of the clock.*)

SACHA: He's going to die, he's not immortal and then life will change.

LYDIA: (*Frightened*) What on earth is the child saying? From where did you get such ideas?

SACHA: From here of course. From you. Everyone here knows very well that everyone has got to die. On the Continent they are so scared they believe he may be an exception.

(GRICHA *paces round the room like an animal in a small cage.*)

IGOR: What he says is not stupid, not stupid at all. May heaven protect you, Sacha. We must be going now. It has done me a lot of good to see you, Sacha. Perhaps somebody like you can bear witness. It's very important for us to have a witness. And you are right – he's not immortal, with his arteries thickening with so much blood – not *his* blood needless to say – the blood of others. But maybe it comes to the same thing – phhh!

SACHA: What's more, he's old. Seventy-two.

GRICHA: (*Suddenly stops pacing*) Power is an aphrodisiac. Georgians live a long time – with their mountains and their yoghurts and red peppers . . .

LYDIA: It's late, late, we really must be going.

(IGOR, *lost in his thoughts, does not stir.*)

Igor Issaievitch, there will be all the chairs to stack after the film.

(*He still does not move.* LYDIA *takes his hand gently.*)

Igorik, come on, dear.

IGOR: Yes, I'm coming.

(IGOR *starts to hum the waltz. The two of them leave.* SACHA *and* GRICHA *sit down on the same two chairs as at the beginning of the scene. The small table between them.*)

GRICHA: Annissimov – Avevtchenko – Alice, yes, Alice is a Christian name. Still, you can see the logic. Annissimov – Avevtchenko – the cunning bastards.

(GRICHA *takes the moustache out of his pocket.* SACHA *fetches a box of matches from the stove, strikes one, and leans across the table with the idea of setting fire to the moustache.* GRICHA *blows out the match.*)

You – you understand nothing! You are just a tourist here! Nothing more than a tourist.
(*He begins to pull the imaginary chain, but this time it is he himself who stands up and sits down. His voice is no longer playful, but violent, bordering on hysteria.*)
Up! Down! Up! There's no end to it, it goes on and on, everything starts again, when it is over, it starts again at the beginning – be–ginn–ing, be–ginn–ing. (*Shouting but, by force of habit, prudently so that he cannot be heard in the street*) The in–ex–or–ab–le hell of ge–og–ra–phy.

ACT THREE

SCENE I

About a fortnight later. Evening. The days are getting shorter. It is nearly September. ERNST, DACHA, SACHA, *sitting at the table are in the middle of a conversation.*

SACHA: . . . when I was there, I understood better what Igor Issaievitch was saying about the silence. And I understood something about myself, about my fears. Can you get rid of fears? I don't think so. You have to make a place for them, and then keep them in their place. It's normal to be frightened, isn't it? What's dangerous is when fears break free, then there's panic. It's as if you have to make a room for every one of your fears . . . with a window and a door.

DACHA: Yes . . . yes . . . yes.

ERNST: What did they talk about, your geologists?

SACHA: About the Cenozoic era which lasted seventy million years. They were palaeontologists, Ernst Moisseevitch. And do you know what they had just discovered? A mammoth – a giant mammoth in perfect condition. He looked as if he were alive yesterday, fresh as a daisy. I brought back a present for you.

(SACHA *fetches a parcel from his room.* ERNST *and* DACHA *exchange amused glances.*)

(*Holding out the parcel to* ERNST) It's for you.

ERNST: (*Taking it and then giving it to* DACHA) Really for me?

DACHA: (*Carefully unwrapping the paper and the cotton-wool*) What on earth is it?

(*She holds the object up.*)

SACHA: A mammoth's tooth!

DACHA: It isn't, I can't believe it!

(*She holds it out at arm's length, near* ERNST*'s mouth.*)

Smile, Ernst! Smile and show us your teeth!

(ERNST *gives an enormous grin. Everyone laughs.*)

ERNST: Did you know mammoths used their tusks as snow ploughs? They were well adapted to their habitat.

DACHA: Smile, mammoth! Show us all your teeth!

ERNST: (*Smiling*) By the way, there's no more toothpaste – not even in *their* shop. Deliveries have stopped. (*To* SACHA) Try to send us some from Leningrad. (*Takes out of his pocket a bundle of bank notes tied up with a piece of string.*) This is the money for your ticket. At the latest you should get it for next Friday.

DACHA: Almost a week.

ERNST: That way you'll be there for the beginning of term, and have time to sort out your books. And don't forget to send a telegram to your aunt tomorrow, as soon as you know the time of your plane.

DACHA: From the house to the school is just two tram stops, isn't it?

SACHA: When it's fine, I walk.

ERNST: Micha will find the means to get you to the airport. The weather forecasts are good. They're not predicting the fog till the end of September this year. The planes won't be grounded. You'll easily get a place, but be good and book it tomorrow.

(SACHA *goes back into his room and returns with a long-handled broom – as is used for sweeping streets.*)

DACHA: (*Laughing*) And what's this magic? We've got a broom, Sacha, you know that.

SACHA: The palaeontologists had ten brooms like this! An administrative error! So they gave me one.

(ERNST *has been checking the money and is now retying the string around the wad of notes.*)

ERNST: For brushing the mammoth's teeth, perhaps, Sacha? . . . When I was a child there was a toothpaste which smelt of cucumbers. Pale green in colour. Odd how your broom brings that back to me. No – not so much – it was the gardener sweeping the leaves, he had a broom which seemed to me to be as tall as a tree . . . Perhaps on the Continent they still produce a toothpaste that smells a little artificially of cucumbers?

SACHA: (*Preoccupied*) Maybe . . .

(DACHA *fetches the triptych, places it on the table, opens it – its back to the audience.*)

DACHA: Will you do something for me, Sachinka? One day when you have time, walk across the bridge and go and look at these three pictures in the Hermitage. Look at them for yourself – and for us. When I got my White Pass and I found this room for us to live in, in the way you have seen, and the way we have to live, well, it was then that I found these three reproductions, and they were the first present, real present, which I ever gave to Ernst.

(SACHA *looks carefully at the images, then shuts the triptych.*)

SACHA: I'm not going back to Leningrad. Not for the Hermitage. Not for some toothpaste.

ERNST: You have to be serious, Sacha.

SACHA: I'm staying here.

ERNST: Sacha, arguments are not good for your mother's blood pressure . . .

DACHA: Please, Sacha.

SACHA: I'm staying.

ERNST: Let us examine the situation carefully. You've spent your holidays here, you've seen a lot – even a mammoth! You have found your mother after fifteen years . . .

DACHA: We'll see each other again soon, we'll spend many, many, many days together.

ERNST: You can come back next year.

SACHA: When?

ERNST: The 4th of July 1953!

DACHA: You'll have finished school by then, we'll have plenty of time to talk, to talk about your future.

SACHA: What future?

ERNST: We'll be able to discuss, you'll be able to talk with us, about what you want to do with your life.

SACHA: (*Calmly*) What I am – whether I want it or not – has already been decided, once and for all, by my mother and father.

(*Silence.* DACHA, *visibly troubled, goes to the 'kitchen corner' by the sink.*)

ERNST: (*Speaking precisely but with much hesitation*) If what you mean, if what you have just said means that Dacha, your mother, and Serioja, your father, both of them belonging to the population of Zeks, if what you mean is that you, as their son, risk, as a consequence of being their son, to be marked for life, you are partly right, and we must admit it, but only partly right. Only partly right, Sacha, because I believe that a man's life is not really determined by the accident of his birth in a particular place during a particular year to two particular parents – all these particulars are what *they* note in their files – this counts for a lot, but everything I have seen leads me to believe that the accident of birth is not what finally counts.

DACHA: We have so few choices and, day after day, we choose. Is it a different way of choosing?

ERNST: Each one of us comes into the world with her or his unique possibility – which is like an aim, or, if you wish, almost like a law. The job of our lives is to become – day by day, year by year, more conscious of this aim so that it can at last be realized. If we want to, we can know it. Magadan and Leningrad – geography and history, parents and occupation, it's all accidental. A question of chance. But to beat the accidental, Sacha, is to respect the law and to achieve the aim.

SACHA: And in what paragraph is your wonderful law inscribed?

ERNST: (*Smiling*) The unfindable one. (*Pause.*) It's inscribed differently in each one of us – inscribed by God at the same moment as he gave us life . . .

(*Enter* GRICHA, *downcast as we have never seen him. He takes a chair at the table.*)

DACHA: Some tea?

(GRICHA *shakes his head.*)

What's the matter with you?

GRICHA: Fucked up. I can't sleep. Can't sleep a wink. I just lie on my back thinking. I don't want to be tactless, last thing I want to do – but I've discovered something which concerns us all . . .

(*The door is flung open and a* YOUNG WOMAN *rushes in.*

Apparently drunk. Dishevelled hair. Unknown to anyone present. Her voice is high and excited. Her words are slow at first.)

YOUNG WOMAN: Can someone help me? Please someone. They told me there might be a doctor here. Is there? Is there a doctor in the house? You see, they laugh!

(*She comes towards the table like a blind person.* DACHA *and* ERNST *get to their feet.*)

ERNST: I'm a doctor. What is it you're complaining of?

YOUNG WOMAN: (*Faster*) Where have they taken him, tell me, doctor, where? Can't you, doctor, can't you give me back my life? He's disappeared, gone, and his shoes are still under the bed. Where have they put his feet, doctor? . . . A full bottle of red rose-hips for his birthday. I poured out glasses for him and for me, and I drank for him and for me. It was going to be his birthday today. How many steps? Thirty-eight? He'll never be late now. Now he'll never be early. And I can't go to the port bar to bring him home. On my two feet, alone, I can't keep going, for how long, doctor?

(DACHA *places a chair behind the* YOUNG WOMAN *and makes her sit.* DACHA *herself stays standing behind the chair, and motions with her head so that* ERNST *sits down where he was before. NB When* DACHA *begins to calm the* YOUNG WOMAN, DACHA*'s face will not be directly visible to the audience.*)

It would be easier with one foot, wouldn't it? It would be over sooner. When he came home, we drank a glass each and we had four feet. He said: Forget it, forget it, hushaby, I love your freckles, and I said: I want a child . . . that'll make six feet. Do you know, doctor, how deep it is between the double windows? One foot. I look for him there, between the windows.

(DACHA *places her hands gently on the* YOUNG WOMAN*'s back.*)

He has a habit of scratching his right ear with his left hand. (*Imitates the gesture.*) If you see him, doctor, you'll recognize him. Tell him I've got a squirrel for him, no, two, two. How do they cut off their own hands? How do they open their own veins? (*Begins to become calmer.*) Don't think about it, he told me, have a drink and forget it, hushaby. Yes, yes. Don't think, no. They've taken him, yes. They've broken my heart, yes. (*Almost calm*) It is so so hard to say yes. (*She leans her head back against* DACHA*'s breast.*) To what office should I go with a pain like mine to get its papers? (*Pause.*) If I find a squirrel, I'll kill it. Two squirrels I'm going to kill, to make him a chapka. (*Gets up and walks steadily towards the door.*) He lost his chapka last spring. Yes, yes, he must have a chapka, yes. To keep warm, you should know that, you need two squirrels.

(*She is just about to leave. No one has moved.*)

GRICHA: His name please?

YOUNG WOMAN: The same as mine.

(*Exit* YOUNG WOMAN. DACHA, *visibly exhausted, grasps the back of the chair on which the* YOUNG WOMAN *was sitting.* ERNST *and* SACHA *lead her to the bed where she sits down.* ERNST *puts his arm round her shoulders and sits beside her. The corner where the bed is is only half lit.* SACHA *returns to the table where* GRICHA *is still sitting.*)

GRICHA: Forget it! Forget it! It's not bad advice. Soon it'll be our turn. I know what's happening, I know everything now. Once, the first time, at the beginning, they accused us, they brought a case against each one of us, they forced us to confess, there was a prosecution. This time it's much simpler, as simple as the ABC. They need labour and they're not getting enough from the Continent, and so they're taking us back inside, and it doesn't matter what Article we were arrested under. This time it's by alphabetical order. Last week it was the As, this week it's the Bs, it's as simple as the ABC . . . A . . . B . . . C.

DACHA: Poor kid! (*Nods towards the door.*) It's already an eternity.

GRICHA: Next week it will be the Cs, then the Ds . . . Between their alphabetical order and their geography they have us well and truly fucked.

SACHA: Sshhh . . .

GRICHA: (*Getting to his feet*) As for you, Sachinka, listen to your old friend for once. Get the hell out of here, as soon as you can make it. It'll be one worry less for your mother.

SACHA: There are three people living on this planet whom I really care about. They're my world, and they are here.

(GRICHA *leaves almost on tiptoe.* ERNST *and* DACHA *are still on the bed.* SACHA, *very quietly, goes to where the door of his room is leaning against the wall, picks it up, carries it to the door frame and lowers it on to its hinges.*)

DACHA: What is it you're doing, Sacha?

SACHA: I'm staying here!

(*The door is on its hinges.*)

And if you want to get rid of me, you'll have to carry me out tied to my door!

(*Immobility. Then* ERNST *takes* DACHA *by the hand and leads her to the middle of the stage where she sits down on the chair left by the* YOUNG WOMAN. *She faces the audience.* ERNST *stands formally behind the chair and* SACHA *joins them. They pose, stiffly, as for a family photograph. Artificial lighting emphasizes this effect. Perhaps there should be a 'flash'.*)

SERIOJA: (*Voice reading from his letter, from back of auditorium*) 'He didn't foresee a third category: somebody who is neither newborn, nor old, neither living nor dead . . . but who has a memory.'

SACHA: (*Impersonal voice, no gestures or movement*) I know every square millimetre of your body, astonishingly and eternally.

ERNST: (*Straight to audience, without gestures*) You had pneumonia when you arrived. You were just one among all the other feverish and exhausted bodies. One more. So many arrivals and departures, and many of those departing were leaving on the longest journey. Some get better, others don't, and the difference between them is so slight. You, you slept all the time, Dachenka. I had four hours' sleep a night. Little by little you slept less. And when you could get out of bed, you worked as my nurse. Once I said to you: If all nurses were like you . . . and you laughed and replied: I was born under the sign of Pisces. In the woman's ward of the hospital of Camp number 102, you slept in the bed against the wall by the door, and my bed was just on the other side of the wall. One night, you made your way out of the ward, and you came to me, your hands smelling of hay and honey. It was the winter of 'forty-four.

DACHA: (*Immobile*) No, Eric, it was already the month of April 'forty-four. Even with the snow, the air smelt of spring.

SCENE 2

Two or three days later. Evening light outside. DACHA *is wearing her smart dress (as at Sacha's arrival) and high-heeled shoes. She is ironing. Beside her on the table two piles of clothes already ironed.* SACHA *is lying on his stomach on her bed. Whilst reading he cracks hazel-nuts with his teeth, and eats them. The curtain rises on silence – except for the noise of the nuts and the vague sounds of the town through the window.*

DACHA: Katya's expecting you any day. Read her letter.
(*She leaves the table and places the letter on the book* SACHA *is reading.*)
Perhaps it's just as well you haven't told her yet.

SACHA: (*Absorbed by what he is reading*) Later . . .
(DACHA *continues ironing.*)

DACHA: You shouldn't break the nuts with your teeth.

SACHA: Do you want me to break them with your teeth?

DACHA: Find a stone.

SACHA: Takes too long. Why don't you let me read?

DACHA: When you see Katya, please tell her about Ernst.

SACHA: Why do you go on? I've never seen anyone so pigheaded.
The two of you, you and Ernst, you make a real pair.
Leningrad is over, finished. Do you see?
(*Silence.* DACHA *arranges what she has ironed on the shelves in the cupboard.*)

DACHA: Look, Sachinka, you have to look now – here on this side are your things.
(SACHA *continues to read.*)
Do you want to make me angry? Listen for once!
(SACHA *looks up.*)
Here are Ernst's things – here are yours. Sheets and pillowcases are on the top shelf.

SACHA: Why do you tell me all that? I know it.
(*He starts to read again.*)

DACHA: Ernst can't tell the difference between a clean shirt and a dirty one.

SACHA: For others yes, for himself, no.

DACHA: He's like a baby. You must explain to him. (*Searches in the cupboard.*) Where in God's name have I hidden my winter boots? Where? (*Takes out a dress on a coat-hanger and hangs it on top of the open cupboard door.*) This dress could do with an iron.

(*She takes a pile of clothes from the cupboard and puts them on the table. She still hasn't found her boots. Kneeling on the floor, she pulls out a suitcase from under the bed on which* SACHA *is lying.*)

Where for heaven's sake?

SACHA: What's it you're looking for?

DACHA: My winter boots.

SACHA: We're only at the end of the month of August and she's looking for her winter boots!

DACHA: They need repairing and Ernst has found a man who can do it. If he takes them tonight, they'll be ready in ten days.

(*Two sharp knocks on the door.* SACHA *sits up.* DACHA *still on her knees, buries her head in her son's lap. For an instant.*)

Who is it?

(DACHA *gets to her feet, opens the door. Enter two* BRUISE. SACHA *standing by the door of his room.* BRUISE I *hands* DACHA *a blue paper – she glances at it.*)

BRUISE I: It's for a routine check-up.

DACHA: (*Giving back the paper*) It was always just for a check-up. (*Smiling*) No?

(BRUISE 2 *goes to the open cupboard and searches between the clothes, throwing some on the floor. He finds the wad of bank notes tied with string.*)

BRUISE 2: (*Throwing the packet on the table at which* BRUISE I *is already seated*) And this – what is it?

DACHA: (*In the middle of the room, standing, calm*) Some money. In fact, the money for my son's return ticket to Leningrad – I applied for, and received the authorization for him to spend his school holidays here. He's leaving in a few days.

BRUISE 2: We'll see.

(BRUISE I *examines the wad of money which his colleague has thrown on the table.* BRUISE 2, *having finished with the cupboard, now goes to the bookshelf and finds the letter from Serioja. During the search, when nothing is being said, we hear the mechanism of the alarm clock.)*

(*Throwing the letter on the table*) And this document, what is it?

DACHA: A letter from my husband – postmarked Vorkouta.

BRUISE I: (*Examining the letter*) It seems then that you have two husbands.

DACHA: I don't understand.

BRUISE I: It's clear enough. You have one husband here and another in Vorkouta.

(BRUISE 2 *picks up the triptych and puts it on the table.* BRUISE I *opens it and they both look at it together.*)

BRUISE 2: A religious object, used for worship. Are you a Baptist?

DACHA: Baptist! Why on earth should I be a Baptist any more than you?

BRUISE I: You believe in God.

DACHA: I don't see the connection.

BRUISE 2: It's with this thing here that you say your prayers!

DACHA: Prayers? Why prayers?

BRUISE I: Then explain what you use it for!

DACHA: (*Calm, approaching the table and standing behind the* BRUISE, *speaking with the slow intonation of a museum guide*) On your left, you see a Madonna by Leonardo da Vinci, the so-called *Litta Madonna*, fifteenth century; in the middle you can see *The Flight into Egypt* by Nicolas Poussin, seventeenth century, French school; on your right you find *David's Farewell to Jonathan*, painted by Rembrandt, seventeenth century, Dutch. Some historians maintain that it represents David's reconciliation with Absalom, the gesture of David does perhaps suggest a reconciliation rather than a farewell. All three pictures are to be found in the Hermitage Museum in Leningrad.

BRUISE 2: We're confiscating it.

(*He looks at his colleague for approval.*)

DACHA: No! You have no right.

BRUISE I: How did you come by these treasures? Were they stolen?

SACHA: It was me. I brought these pictures from Leningrad for my mother.

BRUISE I: Did you buy them? How much did you pay for them?

SACHA: I tore them out of the art magazine *Iskustvo*. If you look carefully, you'll see they're cheap reproductions.

BRUISE 2: (*Peering close into the triptych*) They're icons and disgusting ones! Look. Look at her. Her tits are outside.

DACHA: Even you probably fed at your mother's breast.

BRUISE I: (*Folding and unfolding the wooden triptych*) You're all the same, all of you 58s. You think you're clever. But I wasn't born yesterday either. This object smells of priests. (*Turns round to address* SACHA) As for you, citizen, you'd better leave without another word.

DACHA: Please give me just five minutes. In five minutes I'll be ready, there's no need for anger, nobody is tricking you, nobody is trying to get the better of you. My son is leaving in a few days, and I'll be leaving in five minutes with you. (*Holds out her arms towards them.*) You can be sure, I am ready, everything is ready, there's no need for anything more.

(*Her arms still extended, her hands rest very lightly on the shoulders of* BRUISE I. *He rises to his feet slowly and both* BRUISE, *almost in slow-motion, move towards the open door where they wait, leaning against the door frame.* DACHA *lays out a large scarf on the table, throws her clothes into it, makes a bundle, ties a knot, and approaches* SACHA.)

Beneath so many closed eyes the sleep of no one.

(*She stuffs the wad of money into his pocket.*)

Take the plane, my boy, from the airport of Magadan. And never forget: it isn't over.

(*She goes to the door, changes into her outdoor shoes and whispers beside the two* BRUISE.)

It isn't over. It's not finished. It's not the end.

(DACHA *leaves, without turning back to look at* SACHA. *The two* BRUISE *shut the door behind them.* SACHA *alone, leaning against the partition wall of his room. We hear the clock. He does not move. Slowly he looks round the room, surveying the disorder. He wipes the back of his hand across his forehead, then he touches both of his thighs. He walks somewhat unsteadily towards the table.*)

SACHA: (*Picking up his father's letter, reinserting it into a book*) And the money, where's it gone? (*Looks on the floor.*) They left it on the table. (*Puts the triptych back into its place.*) Where could it have gone?

(*The corner of the suitcase under the bed catches his eye, he pulls it out, looks inside, holds up something wrapped in newspaper.*)

The boots she was looking for!

(*A boot in each hand, he hesitates, then places them deliberately on the table and goes back to kick the suitcase under the bed. He begins to tidy the wardrobe cupboard. The lights go down.*)

Bastards! 'On this side are your things. Here are Ernst's things.'

(*He continues to tidy and to pick up things from the floor. Lights very low.*)

'Sheets and pillowcases are on the top shelf. You must explain to him. He can't tell the difference between a clean shirt and a dirty one. You must explain to him. He's like a baby.'

(*Silence. Mechanism of the clock. The noise of a key in the door. Suddenly the lights are switched on by* ERNST *who stands in the doorway.*)

ERNST: (*Shouting*) Dacha! Where is Dacha?

(*He approaches* SACHA *by the wardrobe, who, head bowed, says nothing.* ERNST *puts his doctor's bag on the table; from his string bag he takes out a loaf of bread and some potatoes. Then he repeats in a whisper*) Where is Dacha?

SACHA: They came to get her.

ERNST: When?

SACHA: (*Looking at the clock*) An hour ago.

ERNST: How many were they?

SACHA: Two.

ERNST: Did they have a warrant?

SACHA: Yes, a blue bit of paper.

ERNST: What did they ask about?

SACHA: The triptych.

ERNST: Nothing else?

SACHA: Father's letter – they found it.
ERNST: Only that?
SACHA: The money. (*Feels in his pockets, finds the wad of notes.*) What a fool. It was there all the time.
ERNST: Keep the money. What did she take with her?
SACHA: What she had.
ERNST: (*Looking at the boots on the table and the dress on the coat hanger*) She didn't take these.

(*He takes the boots off the table and places them carefully on the floor beneath the dress. He sits down, pulls up a chair for* SACHA.)

Sit down here.

(SACHA *sits.*)

You see, now, don't you, you have to leave.
SACHA: (*Head bowed*) I'll wait for her.
ERNST: Yes, in Leningrad.
SACHA: No, I'll wait here. And you?
ERNST: I've a bed at the hospital.
SACHA: If I stay, you'll have a home every night.
ERNST: (*Sceptically*) A home?
SACHA: (*Drily*) It's something, isn't it?

(ERNST *puts his head between his hands and sobs.* SACHA *looks at him for a moment and then, out of tact, tiptoes into his room, leaving the door open. We see the light by his bedside through the door. Mechanism of clock . . .* ERNST *raises his head.*)

ERNST: Sacha . . . Sacha.

(*He looks around the room. Gets up slowly. Puts the chair back under the table. Walks – limping more obviously than usual – towards Sacha's door.*)

I don't want to disturb you.
SACHA: 'I don't want to disturb you.' Sometimes you make me laugh, Ernst Moisseevitch!

(ERNST *enters Sacha's room. From now on we hear their voices but do not see them. The lights in the main room go down. Only the light in Sacha's room remains.*)

ERNST: Tomorrow you must put your name down for the school. You know where it is?
SACHA: Yes, I know.

ERNST: You must send a telegram to your aunt.

SACHA: We must get her winter boots repaired.

ERNST: I'll take them with me tonight. Take care of the money – it should be enough for three months.

SACHA: We'll take great care . . .

(The image of the 'imagined' family photo – Dacha, Ernst, Sacha – taken during the first scene of this act, is projected on to the twelve square metres of hardboard, the walls of Sacha's room. At first the image is out of focus, gradually it sharpens, as the light through the doorway diminishes. The sharp image is held for twenty seconds before the lights go down.)